# The Upside of Undertaking

# The Upside of Undertaking

## Catherine Olen

Illustrated by
Todd Wiessenhutter

Schiffer Publishing Ltd

4880 Lower Valley Road, Atglen, Pennsylvania 19310

# Dedication

This book is lovingly dedicated to my husband, Jeff, for his unending love and support in my obsession with celebrity grave hunting and my daughter, Brooke, for her patience and hours of assistance trekking through cemeteries to find the next gravesite.

*All text by author*
*Illustrations by Todd Wiessenhutter*

Schiffer Books are available at special discounts for bulk purchases for sales promotions or premiums. Special editions, including personalized covers, corporate imprints, and excerpts can be created in large quantities for special needs. For more information contact the publisher:

Published by Schiffer Publishing Ltd.
4880 Lower Valley Road
Atglen, PA 19310
Phone: (610) 593-1777; Fax: (610) 593-2002
E-mail: Info@schifferbooks.com

For the largest selection of fine reference books on this and related subjects,
please visit our web site at **www.schifferbooks.com**
We are always looking for people to write books on new and related subjects.
If you have an idea for a book please contact us at the above address.

This book may be purchased from the publisher.
Include $5.00 for shipping.
Please try your bookstore first.
You may write for a free catalog.

In Europe, Schiffer books are distributed by
Bushwood Books
6 Marksbury Ave.
Kew Gardens
Surrey TW9 4JF England
Phone: 44 (0) 20 8392-8585; Fax: 44 (0) 20 8392-9876
E-mail: info@bushwoodbooks.co.uk
Website: www.bushwoodbooks.co.uk

Designed by Mark David Bowyer
Type set in UniversityRoman Bd BT / New Baskerville BT

ISBN: 978-0-7643-3586-0
Printed in the United States of America

# Contents

# Acknowledgments

**F**irst and foremost, I thank my husband, Jeff, for his support during the writing of this book.

My thanks to Todd Wiessenhutter for her talents putting together wonderful illustrations.

Many thanks to Schiffer Publishing for taking on this project and supporting my efforts.

Lastly, to all of the families and co-workers during my years in the funeral industry; there are too many to mention—thank you for your participation in creating these glorious memories.

# Introduction

**"Y**ou're writing a book about what?" This was the reaction from most of my family and friends when I made the grand announcement that I was planning to write a book about my experiences in the funeral industry.

To my way of thinking, it should not have come as any surprise to them that I would pursue this venture, particularly since I had been telling the stories found between the covers of this book for years at family gatherings to the giggles and incredulous looks of relatives. After nearly a decade in the funeral industry and fifteen years of celebrity grave-hunting as a personal hobby, some would consider me an authority of sorts on matters pertaining to death. Small talk for me generally consists of what some might consider ghoulish and macabre stories from my daily life and the lives of so many friends and colleagues I've met over the years.

I love sharing not only my own stories, but also the wonderfully touching tales of the great celebrity lives and deaths I've had the privilege of hearing about from so many others in the funeral industry.

I have been sharing these experiences for so long that the stories feel like old friends that love to come and visit. So often when I have had the delight of meeting someone new, the definitive icebreaker would follow the trite questions, "So what do you do for a living?"

"I am a grave hunter," I reply mischievously, watching closely for the inevitable reaction.

I enjoy the subtle double-take or the jaw-dropping surprise when the words sink in. I cannot recall a time that my new friends didn't have an arm's length of questions about how I got involved with this unique profession.

Eventually, I realized that people really do want to be able to feel at ease around the subject of death…if perhaps only subconsciously. I've been witness to the reactions of the public when a celebrity passes away, the constant need for information seeming insatiable. A universal grief seems to overwhelm society when notables pass away. This is even more the case when tragedy strikes and takes a promising young actor or actress from us too soon.

Within these pages, there are some very interesting factoids on the nature of the human condition and some plain old foolishness thrown in for good measure. If I can make you laugh or ease your mind so that you can look at the experience of death and memorials a little differently, then my job here is complete.

I hope you enjoy reading this as much as I enjoyed writing it for you.

# A Day in the Life of a Mortician

Seldom in our busy lives do we ever sit down and think about death itself, let alone imagine that anything remotely funny could be associated with the process of memorializing and burying the dead. Let me assure you, there are more opportunities for funny mishaps and rib-tickling incidents than you could ever imagine. For those in the funeral industry, the majority of funerals are exactly the same as weddings, one just blending into the next in a cookie-cutter fashion, each person doing much the same as the one before. Ninety-seven percent of the hundreds of funerals I was a part of were exactly this way for me (and now for you, too), but fortunately, there were those rare occasions that something truly memorable and usually silly occurred.

I promise you that the truth is much stranger than fiction. If I hadn't had these experiences myself, I would never believe even half of what is written here.

# You Want Her to Wear What?

I was making arrangements for a family whose mother had just passed away. One of the last things I tell the family is to bring in whatever they would like to see the deceased dressed in at the service. Very seldom does the family think to bring the clothing to our first meeting. Usually, they leave and then take great pains to pick something that Mom would have wanted to wear and something she would be pretty in, returning later in the day with the clothing. When I asked this particular family about the clothing, they lit up and said, "Oh, we've got it here!"

I hadn't noticed any of the loved ones carrying anything, so I sat quietly while the daughter pulled out a very small package from her purse. I watched curiously while she pulled a very sheer, flimsy black robe and short night-gown from the package and held it up for me to see.

There are some moments in your life that there really are no words for; this was definitely one of them. The daughter had a look of pure joy on her face as she held the garments up for inspection, and the rest of the family members did not even flinch. Thankfully, she broke the silence, explaining, "Mom decided a long time ago that she wanted to be buried in her favorite negligee."

Now let me stop here for a moment and tell you that up until that very moment, I had felt like I was a seasoned professional in the funeral industry. I had put together hundreds of services and memorials for families and thought I had been through every situation. Boy, was I wrong!

I sat for a few very long and uncomfortable moments looking at the negligee and the family before asking the question I wasn't sure I wanted an answer to: "Is there anything else to go with this?" To which the casual reply was, "No, she loved wearing this and made sure we knew this was all she wanted on."

At that point, I had to double-check the arrangements we had just finished making to see if the family wanted an open or closed casket. Sure enough, they requested an open casket. I had visions of the looks of horror on the faces of the guests as they walked to the front of the chapel, full of reverence and grief, only to discover Mom in her casket looking like a high-priced call girl with nothing left to the imagination.

In my career, there were very few times I ever denied a family their wishes at the funeral. Literally, I could probably count on two fingers the times I had to say no to a family. I sat for a few more uncomfortable moments trying to wrack my brain for the words to explain to this nice family why we needed to be a little more appropriate with this clothing. I promise you that no one wants to see what can only be described as two empty wallets hanging from the torso of the deceased!

Well, on this particular day, I felt like I had been touched by an angel as the words came from my mouth, explaining that the state required the deceased to be dressed in something that would ensure no leakage from the loved one. Now, I don't know if there are any state regulations about burial clothing, but it sure sounded good at the time, and the family never batted an eye as they left to bring in something a little more appropriate for Mom. I still took the original garments they brought in and assured the family that they would be put into the casket with Mom in case she wanted a quick change of clothes.

# First Trip to the Coroner's Office

When I started my career, I worked as a receptionist at a local funeral home, getting on-the-job training so I could move up to arranging services for the families. On an average week, we would get anywhere from six to ten calls from the county coroner's office asking us to pick up a body they were finished with. When this occurred, two of the staff would load the gurney into the van and would return with the deceased.

On this particular rainy day in October, we were very short-staffed and loaded with services, so it was just me and one of the funeral directors in the office. One of my new colleagues, Kristine, informed me that I would have to go with her to the coroner because she was picking up two bodies, a man and his wife, whose lives had been claimed in a car accident, and she couldn't handle them alone. I hesitated for a moment as I considered what she was asking me to do. I was just a receptionist; I didn't want to deal with dead bodies (pretty strange thoughts for someone who had decided on a career in the funeral industry). After a moment of soul-searching, I agreed to go and help out. We loaded the two gurneys and were off to the coroner's office. We entered the loading area, where I assisted Kristine with unloading the equipment, and then we walked in the door.

I was pleasantly surprised to see how clean and orderly everything was as we entered the facility. Gleaming polished doors and counter tops, a large whiteboard on the wall with names and statistical information, and rows of neat paperwork waiting for the mortuaries to pick up.

To my great relief, there was not a dead body in sight! A portly man came out of the office, and my associate handed him the paperwork. After taking a cursory glance at it, he pointed to a large white door at the end of the hall. Kristine turned to me and said, "Okay, let's go into the cooler." I stood there with what must have been a look of horror on my face because she laughed and said, "Come on! No time like the present to get it over with."

I followed her to the hall with no small amount of trepidation. The man dressed in a white lab coat swung the door open, and a blast of cool air hit me. Inside was a huge sterile room with row after row of bodies covered with sheets or in body bags. Kristine just walked in and started looking at the tags to find the two we were taking with us. I stood there frozen in grim fascination as she casually made her selections as if she were picking up her dry cleaning.

"Okay, here they are. Help me load them."

"What do I do?" I asked, like I couldn't figure it out for myself.

She looked at me, exasperated. "Just take the feet, and help me move him."

Unfortunately, this particular body had the feet sticking out the end of what looked like a garment bag you would see pulled over a suit when you buy it from the department store. The important part to note about this is that nothing was covering the legs from the knee down. Kristine counted to three, and we both lifted him up.

As we were doing this, I looked down and noticed that the left leg drooped in a very unnatural fashion. Using keen power of deduction, I quickly realized that the leg had been severed almost all the way through. I'm sure the blood must have drained from my face. After rolling her eyes at my startled scream, Kristine had to place her "end" on the gurney and then move around the table to finish the job for me. Mercifully, she placed a cover over the stretcher once the body was in place.

"Don't worry. You'll be okay. Just one more to go." She tried to reassure me.

All I wanted to do was sit down for a minute before the floor came up to meet me, but like a trooper, I went ahead and moved to the next one.

"You take the head this time," she said, obviously trying to ease my concern.

"Thanks," I said with some relief. I walked to the head of the deceased, we both lifted, and something heavy fell to the bottom of the bag. Fortunately, I couldn't see what it was. But being all too familiar with autopsy procedures, I knew that the cranium cap must have slid off the top of the head as I lifted the body. That was it for me! Once again, Kristine had to come to the rescue. She tersely told me, "You go sit in the van while I load them in the back."

"Okay," was the only thing I could mutter at this point for fear my breakfast would be coming back to haunt me at any moment.

I sat in the front of the van as we made the drive back to the office in silence. There are moments in your life that call for introspection; this was definitely one of those moments for me. I kept asking myself, *What in the HELL are you doing here? Who does this voluntarily day after day?* We arrived at the office, and one of the embalmers helped Kristine unload, which was a relief for both of us. I went quietly back to my desk.

# Body At The Top

Another of my experiences picking up a dead body was a few weeks after my first incident. Feeling much more a seasoned professional, I had assisted on several calls going to houses *and* hospitals to escort these recently passed persons to the mortuary for preparation.

During one of the hottest weeks in August, we received a call from the Long Beach police to come pick up the body of a woman who had died in her apartment a few days prior, but the neighbors had just discovered her due to the smell emanating from her apartment.

We immediately loaded the van with the gurney and other equipment we would need and took off to the address provided. When we arrived at the site, we discovered that the body in question was in fact on the third floor of an ancient apartment complex in downtown with very narrow stairways and no elevator. While climbing the stairs to get to the third floor, we had to turn the gurney sideways just to get it up the stairs so the questions was raised as to how we were going to get back down the stairs with a body.

When we entered the apartment, the stench of dead flesh was immediately noticeable and the police officers present already had all of the windows open in an attempt to provide a little fresh air. We entered the bedroom and the scene we found was beyond anything we could have anticipated.

The deceased had died in her bed approximately four to five days before. During this time, the heat of the summer had created advanced deterioration to the body. I must stop at this point to tell you, there is nothing worse on earth than the smell of a rotting dead body in the heat of summer; it is an odor that will stay with you for the rest of your life.

The other piece of the puzzle was that this woman was over 350 pounds. Something the police neglected to mention when they called us to pick her up. Now we really were going to need creativity to get her out of her house, let alone down the stairs. We donned our masks and gloves preparing to get to work and surveyed the situation. We decided sliding her into the gurney would be the best plan with each of us on opposite sides of the bed as there was no way we could lift her.

As we approached the bed in the cramped little room, we set up the gurney and made our first attempt to slide her from the bed. We gave the obligatory one, two, three, and Charlie pulled while I pushed as hard as I could. To my surprise, the body moved quite easily but, unfortunately, not all of her body moved at the same time. When I looked down, I realized that only her stomach actually moved while the rest of the body had stayed stationary, as if glued to the bed. I looked at my colleague and he shook his head at me and said two words, "Skin slip."

Here I stop again to explain this phenomenon. During the decomposition process, liquid builds up under the skin while the body is resting; this causes the skin to break away from connective tissue, bone, and muscle so the skin moves freely. While the description *sounds* unpleasant, imagine seeing it firsthand.

At this point we looked over at the policemen who were watching us intently, but failing to offer any help with the situation. "How are we suppose to get this person out of here?" I heard Charlie ask them.

"We don't know," said the taller policeman who looked around nervously. "The coroner didn't want her and no one locally would come when we told them the circumstances."

It was all starting to make sense now. We had been conned into coming out on the hottest day of summer to this messy situation with only half the story because no one else wanted to bother with this poor woman.

"We thought about lowering her out the window," stated the second policeman. That would be the spectacle with all of us hoping not to drop her half way down.

Charlie finally decided to call the office and find out what our next plan would be. I waited not too patiently while he went to the car to call our boss to explain the situation.

What seemed like hours, but was only a few minutes later, Charlie bound up the stairs and into the tiny apartment, announcing that we were going back to the office without our cargo. The Long Beach police would be figuring this one out without us. As we walked out the door with our equipment in hand, Charlie turned back one last time to the stunned police and said, "Next time fellas, make sure the people you call can get the job done."

We never did find out what happened to that poor woman lying in her bed...

When we returned back to the mortuary, my co-workers asked about what happened and why we returned without the body. We explained the circumstances involving the death and the response was utter disbelief.

Years later, I investigated what would happen to someone in this situation out of my own morbid curiosity. It turns out that the medical examiner was ultimately responsible for the body and their staff would have to arrange for the pickup. Once the county is able to get the person out of the home, they appoint a mortuary to have the person cremated and given a proper burial. It is a comfort knowing society has reverence for the citizens of their community when someone is alone in the world.

# Who Was the Grave Meant For?

While all funerals are difficult and sad, when a child passes away it makes the affair much more difficult for everyone involved. Most of the time, you are expecting an elderly relative to go, or there is some warning before someone passes. No matter what the circumstance, with child funerals, everyone is devastated, so you really have to put your best foot forward to ensure the family is cared for properly. This was the case with the latest family we were working with.

The service had been as proper and as perfect as we could expect. All that was left was the graveside service. We loaded the small casket into the hearse and drove to the cemetery with the family in tow. When we arrived, the family was instructed to sit while my partner carried the casket to the gravesite. For those who have not experienced an open gravesite, normally there is a pile of dirt next to an open hole in the ground. Chairs are located on the opposite side of the grave from the dirt. I noticed that there was no dirt and made the assumption that the cemetery crew would be digging the grave after the service. This was not the case at this particular cemetery. They had dug the hole, removed the dirt from the area, and covered the hole, surrounding the area with fake grass. I looked on as my colleague carried the lightweight casket toward the platform. Suddenly, she disappeared to the waist, still holding the box in her hands.

We looked at each other for a moment, horrified and not sure what to do. Then I calmly walked forward, lifted the casket out of her hands, and set it on the pedestal behind her, thinking she would crawl out of the hole while I was busy. When I turned around, she was still standing in the hole, waiting for something to happen. Please note, this whole episode was playing out right in front of the grieving family, their friends, and the clergyman.

I attempted to assist her in getting out of the grave as professionally and with as much dignity as I could muster. Meanwhile, neither of us dared to even glance in the direction of the onlookers. Just about the time we had gotten her out of the grave, I stole a peek and noticed that several of the mourners looked like they were holding their breath. Just then, someone in the crowd could be heard laughing quietly. As you know, laughter is highly contagious, and clearly several people had found the humor, because the giggles quickly spread to the entire crowd and turned into fits of laughter. The family and even the clergyman chuckled. Finally, the crowd pulled themselves together, and the service went on. Afterward, the family came to us and thanked us for our services. I'm sure that years later they were able to laugh and tell others of the day the funeral director fell into the grave and gave everyone some comic relief.

# No Pay For The Third

I've always said that funerals for children were the worst part of my job. The innocence lost is such a tragedy for the family and everyone involved, it takes much more than that of the normal memorial service. Most funeral homes are very sensitive to the needs of these families and offer services for free and nominal cost of caskets, flowers, and burial locations just to ease the burden.

...That is until I met a family late in my career that I have never forgotten. I received a call from this family that they had lost an infant child and would like the child buried with their other children in the infant section of the cemetery.

My first thought was how many children do these people have here? As I completed the call and scheduled the appointment, I told them I would check the records to see if we had any available property and have the information when they arrived.

I entered the vault where we kept the records and sifted through the interment cards until I found the family name with the two other infant burials. The good news, there was a plot available adjacent to the other burials, but the bad news came with a large yellow note pinned to the card that I unfolded to read.

This family had children buried with full services in both 1992 and 1995, but neither time did the family pay for the burial plots or the merchandise for these services. As I explained at the beginning of this story, these fees were nominal but still totaled several hundred dollars in unpaid expenses. At the bottom of the note, in large letters, it stated we were to do no more services for these people until these past-due bills were made current and we would only accept cash payments for any future services.

I sighed to myself knowing this would be another difficult arrangement, but knew I would have to be firm on the stance the mortuary was taking with them to make sure we did not lose more money for a third funeral.

That afternoon, the mother and father arrived for the appointment and I escorted them into my office. I started the arrangement by explaining that I did find a plot near the other two infants they had buried and I was sorry they were experiencing this pain again in their lives.

With that being said, I pulled out the arrangement folders for the other two services and began to explain to the parents that we have no record of payment being made for the first two services and would require these bills to be paid in full prior to any services being scheduled for this child. The couple stared across the desk at me for a few seconds and then asked how much they owed. I gave them the total and then we discussed what type of service they would want for this child. Once we had completed the service folder for the current funeral, I gave them the final total for all three services and they left knowing there would be no service date set until they returned with the money.

I put the folder in the mortuary office to wait until the couple returned.

Several days later I was sitting at my desk when the receptionist called me to come to the lobby immediately; there was a problem.

I hurried down the stairs and found a very large crowd of people filling the foyer of the mortuary with the grieving parents in the center of the throng. I approached the couple and asked what was going on.

There was tall man standing next to the parents, he spoke first. "We are here for the service for this couples' baby," he stated firmly and very loudly. Turns out this man was the pastor of the church and he was going to be in charge of the situation, or so he thought.

Never in my life had I ever been as angry as I was at that moment. We were being manipulated by this family into performing a third service at no cost by intimidating me with all these people standing around expectantly. The couple was holding each other with their faces down and would not look at me or respond when I asked them to step into my office.

The pastor spoke again, "Just tell us where the service is being held so we can begin," he barked at me.

The hairs on the back of my neck were standing on end and I tried in vain to remain calm as I explained in a clear voice that there were no services scheduled for the child for that day or any day as we had not completed the arrangement. I went on to tell the large crowd that the parents knew this and we still needed to work out payment before any services would be scheduled.

Not to be outdone, the pastor pulled me aside, but still within hearing distance of everyone present and asked me if I would like to explain to the *Orange County Register* that the mortuary was causing this poor family so much grief after losing a child.

At this point, I smiled to myself. This guy was good, but I was better. "Here, allow me to call them for you," I started. "I would love to be interviewed by the paper and explain how a family that had not only lost one child but *three* would have the nerve to pull a stunt like this and try to get away with not paying a third time. How much sympathy do you think the public will have for your grieving family with that on the front page?"

Instantaneously, the expression on old pastors face changed. He knew he would not be able to strong arm me or the mortuary into getting the family what they wanted. Slowly he turned and motioned to the couple. They approached in slow motion with a white-haired woman following them.

When they reached us, they stopped and looked up expectantly. I once again told them that there would be no services until the payment was made for all past and present bills. The white-haired woman came forward aggressively and began to rummage through her purse, all the while cursing under her breath. She shoved a credit card in my hand and told me to put whatever amount was needed on the card. I accepted the card and asked the group to follow me to accounting so we could process their payment.

Meanwhile, people in the lobby had begun moving outside and into the chairs and sofas still waiting for news. I once again told them that even with the payment made today, we did not have a service scheduled, not only that, but we had not even ordered the casket so we had nothing to bury the baby in. They said they understood and we scheduled the service for two days from then.

It was later, sitting in my office, that I sat going over the incident in my head. Could there have been a different way of handling the encounter? Were there really people in this world so cold as to want something for nothing when they had already lost so much? I guess those answers will never be certain for me.

# Even Christmas Isn't Sacred Anymore!

During my tenure in the funeral industry, more often than not, I found myself working on the holidays. Easter, Thanksgiving, Fourth of July—it didn't matter what day of the week it would fall on, I always managed to be scheduled to work.

I was working on Christmas day one year, and it was very quiet. Historically, the holiday work schedule is very quiet. Few, if any, arrangements are made on holidays, but we always had visitors come into the building, asking for directions to gravesites.

Now, in Southern California, Christmastime is usually sunny and warm, and this Christmas was no exception. It was a beautiful eighty degrees, and the cemetery was filled with families coming to put decorations on the graves. I was startled when the phone rang in my office and I was asked to go to the lobby. I walked to the front and found an elderly couple who looked as if the world was about to end.

"We felt we needed to tell you there are people out there stealing the decorations off of the graves!" the woman blurted.

I had heard of and seen incidents of people walking over to another grave and stealing the flowers from it to put on their loved one's grave, so I was not surprised that this would occur even on Christmas. I thanked them for the information and was about to turn away, but I was met with looks of shock from the couple.

"You don't understand! They're stealing everything!"

I asked them where exactly they had seen this, and they said it was happening on the lawn just behind the mortuary building. I quickly ran to the back of the building and out the door, just in time to see a family of four—father, mother, and two small children no more than ten years old—picking up everything they could get their hands on and piling it into the trunk of their car. The father was just lifting a three-foot Christmas tree into the trunk when they spotted me. Before I could even get to the scene of the crime, they had shut the trunk and piled into the car and were gone. Thankfully, I had the presence of mind to get the license plate number before they sped off.

I guess the high cost of the holidays really does catch up with some people!

I went back inside the mortuary and called the local police to investigate the incident. The local police came by and I walked the two police officers to the area of the cemetery where the thefts took place. The two officers looked at each other, then at me with utter disbelief. A look of confusion crossed one officer's face and he said, "I am not sure how much can be done, but we will issue a report. I don't think anyone at the station is going to believe this."

# Locked Away

After a few years of working with families, one service tends to blend into another. This was the case with my latest service. The family came in, selected the services, viewing, chapel service, grave-side, and traditional burial. Nothing out of the ordinary and certainly nothing I couldn't handle.

The day of the viewing was another day just like all the others. The prep team was busy embalming, dressing, and doing hair and makeup. The office staff was typing up death certificates, burial permits, and preparing memorial folders for services. The funeral directors were placing flowers in chapels and getting things organized for the day.

Now, I say everything was completely normal because what happened next was so out of the ordinary, there was no explanation.

The family I had met with just days before had decided on a viewing before the service but failed to inform me that the husband/father in question had made it clear on his deathbed that he did not want any service and was to be quietly cremated. The family felt otherwise and disregarded his request.

We put the body of the deceased in one of the smaller visitation rooms along with the flowers and arranged the furniture so the family would have a comfortable time during the day. About ten minutes before the family was due to arrive, the funeral director assigned to the case walked back to the room to do one final check to make sure everything was perfect and found the door to the room closed. He quickly turned the handle on the door and found it locked.

With minutes remaining, the funeral director walked into the office and ask, "Where are the keys to the visitation rooms?"

"Why? We never lock those doors," said the secretary.

"I know but the door is locked tight and the family is due now."

Unfortunately, there were no keys in the office to the door and the entire staff began to search in vain for the missing keys.

Meanwhile, the family arrived right on time to see their loved one laid out in the casket they had picked out especially for him. I had the unpleasant task of going to the lobby and explaining it would be a few more minutes and asked them to make themselves comfortable while I hurried back to the office to find out if the door was taken care of.

Luck was not on my side that day. As I turned the corner, I found my boss working at the door with a credit card that had been badly mangled in the process. There was the end of a screw driver sticking out of the locking device with the handle broken off from the force of someone trying to break through the lock.

I stopped up short in front of my boss and asked him what I should do next. His response, "Call a locksmith and tell the family to come back later." I watched incredulously as he walked calmly back to his office and shut the door leaving me to do the unthinkable. I asked the receptionist to call a locksmith and tell them it was an emergency while I would go back to tell the family what was really going on.

Walking back to the lobby was the equivalent of what it must feel like for a prisoner to walk the last mile. It takes forever but is over way too quickly. I arrived back into the lobby and the family stood and asked if it was ready. I asked them to take their seats again as I had something I needed to tell them.

I informed them that the visitation room had been accidently locked and the keys were missing so we had called for a locksmith to come but it would be a few minutes before he arrived. I began apologizing to the wife, telling her this had never happened before and how sorry I was for the inconvenience at this time.

The woman stared at me for a moment and then looked around at her family. They all began to laugh as I sat dumbfounded.

"He said he didn't want a service," stated the wife.

"Boy he sure had the last word this time didn't he?" said the daughter wiping away tears of laughter.

The wife looked at me and again laughed before she spoke again. "My husband told us all he did not want any services before he died. We never thought for a minute he would pull something like this, but he locked that door to make sure we didn't have our way."

I felt relief flood my body. The family were completely at ease with the situation and I can't say I wasn't a little convinced that the husband had in fact created the situation. I just wish he had let me in on it somewhere along the way!

# Waking Up Before Her Time

One of the things I discovered early on in my career was that the funeral industry is a high turnover business. This means that many people get in and quickly leave or change employers regularly. I can only assume this is due to the high stress of the industry and people constantly squabbling with each other as tensions rise.

This time we were searching for a new embalmer and hired a seasoned man in his early forties. Dan had worked for one of the large mortuaries and was used to high volume and fast pace. Not the case at our little family mortuary, he found himself sometimes bored and looking for something to do.

This day, we received a call to pick up a body at one of the local nursing homes. These facilities called regularly and we were familiar with the procedures when a death occurred. Unfortunately, Dan was not but wanted to fill his time by going out on the call by himself. Not thinking there would be a problem, the office staff gave him the paper work and sent him on his way.

Being a local call, he would be gone less than an hour so we knew he would return shortly. Ninety minutes later he still had not returned and we had no way of contacting him, this being the time before cell phones. He finally arrived two hours later looking pales and shaky.

He put the body in the cooler and began cleaning the gurney to store it until the next call came. Naturally, we were curious as to what had caused his delay and entered the prep room to find out more.

Dan turned quickly towards me as I entered the room, looking startled.

"Don't sneak up on me!" he shouted.

"I didn't, what happened to you today?" I replied.

"Nothing, I'm fine," he stated too fast and he tried to brush past me. I touched his arm and he shrugged me off as if I were an annoying bug. I followed him out of the prep area and into the back office as he busied himself with putting the paperwork into the folder.

Natural curiosity had others in the office asking why he had taken so long and Charlie teasingly asked, "Did you stop for a burger on the way back?"

Dan suddenly spun around and glared at Charlie like he was ready to strike him. "*No*, just leave me alone," he shouted.

"Hey man, we were only teasing. What happened to you out there?"

Dan lowered his head and finally looked up at us. "You guys won't believe it if I tell you. I went to the nursing home and walked up to the desk looking for Mrs. Smith. The nurse told me to go to room 215 bed B and I would find her there."

At this point, Kristine and I stole a sideways glance at each other. We knew all about nursing homes and how they operated. When you arrived at a facility, you always ask the nursing staff to accompany you to the room to point out exactly which body was the dead one. Truth is, it is not easy to tell if someone is dead or asleep sometimes; and you never wanted to make a mistake and wake some poor elderly person up or, God forbid, pick up the wrong body. Dan continued his story, but I was pretty sure how this one was going to end.

"I went to the room and moved the lady from the bed onto the gurney and strapped her in and covered he with the blanket. Then I wheeled her out and into the van. Got into the driver's seat and started the engine. I was sitting there for a few seconds messing with the radio, then I put it in reverse and looked back to back out. As the van started to move I noticed the radio was not the only thing making noise in the van. I stopped the car and looked around and through the mirrors to see if someone was outside trying to talk to me or if the staff was taking a break. I didn't see anyone but I could hear something. I put the van in gear again and turned to look out the back and suddenly saw the body on the gurney was moving. The head was bobbing up and down and the blanket was squirming. I turned off the van and ran to the back doors. I opened them and uncovered this old woman who was strapped to the gurney screaming like a banshee." I unhooked her and helped her to sit up. She kept screaming at me wanting to know what I was doing and wouldn't shut up. I finally got her off the gurney and back into the building. The staff were yelling at me, saying I was an idiot for not knowing a dead body from a live one."

As Dan continued to rant about his experience, the staff gathered around him were like statues. No one moved or even breathed as we listened, wide-eyed to his tale as it unfolded.

"I finally got the other body on the gurney and out the door, but I was shaking so bad on the way back I almost called to tell you guys I quit," he finished.

There are two unwritten rules in the mortuary industry, never sneak up on the living and if a body moved on you, quit. Eventually that is exactly what he did. I am sure Dan is happily selling insurance in a nice quiet office somewhere far away from nursing homes.

# Don't Drop Anything

Another of my colleagues had a similar experience during her tenure working with me at another mortuary in Los Angeles. I was working in my office on a Saturday, catching up on paperwork and enjoying a quiet moment.

Suddenly, the prep room door burst open and one of the embalmers came racing past my door. I looked up just in time to recognize a glimpse of red hair and the blurred body raced past and called out to Kristine.

I could hear the footsteps coming down the hall back towards me and saw her poke her head into my office. She looked like she had seen a ghost—never a good reference in a funeral home.

She came in and took a seat opposite me, visibly trying to catch her breath.

"What on earth happened?" I asked.

She looked at me for a minute and then told me what had occurred moments before.

"I was working on Mrs. Smith and had just finished dressing her. She was laying on the table as I started to fix her hair according to the picture the family gave us. Her hair was teased so I got the comb and was back combing it when the comb slipped out of my hand and fell on the floor. I bent over to pick it up and someone hit me in the back hard. I knew I was alone in there so I ran out as fast as possible."

"Would you like me to go in there and check it out for you?" I volunteered.

"Well, I'll go, but come with me, okay?"

We got up and opened the large heavy door to the prep area. In all funeral homes there are actually two doors to the prep area. The first door opens into a very wide hallway with another identical door on the opposite side. Once you go through that second door, you are in the actual room. We walked the short expanse to the second door and looked in before entering the room. The scene before us made us both laugh and Kristine sighed with relief when she saw what had actually occurred.

While she was fixing the hair of the deceased, the body lay on the table with her arms at her sides. When Kristine bent down to pick up the comb, she must have brushed against the body and one of the arms fell off the edge of the table and hit her in the back. Evidence of this was the fact that Mrs. Smith's arm was still hanging off the table.

"Do you think you'll be okay?" I asked her now that the shock had worn off.

"Yeah, but I sure hope she doesn't try to help again."

# That's Not My Mother!

Very early in my career of helping families care for the death of a loved one, I received a case from a local nursing home. We picked up the deceased, and the nurse on duty informed us that the daughter was having a difficult time accepting the death. This was nothing new as everyone deals with the loss of a loved one differently, so we are always prepared for the anger and sadness that families experience.

The funeral counselor tried to contact the daughter by phone when he had not heard from her by the end of the work day. He did not receive a call back the next day, so he continued to try to reach her, but he got no response. This was a very strange situation, since we are usually prepared to work with the family members within a few hours of the death.

By the third day, the counselor was getting very concerned as he tried once again to reach someone. This time, there was a voice at the other end of the line. He quickly introduced himself and asked if she could schedule a time for the family to come in. As I sat across from my colleague, I watched as his face became increasingly more confused. Then he hung up the phone and sat quietly for a moment. He looked across at me and shook his head.

"You're not going to believe this," he stated. "She claims the deceased is not her mother. She says that this woman assumed her mother's identity, and she has refused to take care of the arrangements."

Now, this was a new one on us. Never in my career had I heard of a family member who flatly refused to deal with the death. For lack of a better idea, we decided to research the claims further. The first call was to the nursing home. The nurse who answered at the nursing home started chuckling when we began to address the situation with her.

"We tried to tell you that the daughter would not accept the circumstances," she stated, slightly amused.

We checked the records to see if there was any other next of kin that could be contacted and found that the deceased woman had a sister out of state listed as a contact in case of emergency. We contacted this woman in hopes that we could get some assistance in resolving this issue. The sister was deeply troubled to hear of the death and the circumstances revolving around her niece; she agreed to assist with convincing her niece to make the arrangements, although she had not spoken with her for many years. Meanwhile, we were advised to contact the local County Health Department to investigate what could be done in case a family refused to take responsibility for a loved one.

Now, in the state of California, vagrant or homeless persons with no record of next of kin are cremated immediately and the remains kept in storage for several years with the hopes that someone will someday claim the urn. In this case however, the remains sat in cold storage waiting for the legal relative to come take care of her mom. This would not be the case here unfortunately. The daughter continued to insist that the remains were not her mother's and wanted nothing to do with this now or ever. The counselor was left with no other choice but to treat this as a case of vagrancy and cremate without services. We informed the sister of the deceased that she could claim the remains after the legal time limit for the state; she was at least relieved to hear this news.

This would normally be where this story would end, but this would not be the case. Several weeks later, my colleague received a phone call from the daughter, asking what had become of the deceased. Officially, California law stated at that time that a mortuary could not divulge information about the disposal of a body without express permission from the family, so it was with no small amount of pleasure that the counselor told this woman that the disposition of the body was none of her business.

# The Firing Over Cremated Remains

Often during my tenure, I would meet with a family who would want to keep things simple—and, frankly, inexpensive—when it came to dealing with the disposition of a loved one. Cremation is becoming more and more popular because it is much less expensive and easier to deal with than a full service and burial. On this occasion, I met with the wife of an elderly man whom she had been married to for only a brief time. There was a significant age difference, and she seemed to be handling the whole affair with little emotion, very businesslike. Just a simple cremation and she would pick up the urn and take her husband home. The entire process takes about four days to complete, including filing the state-required paperwork. I advised her that I would contact her when the process was complete so she could pick up the remains.

Everything went as planned, and I was able to contact her within three days. She seemed pleased with the expedience and came that day to pick up the urn. I escorted her to my office and then brought her husband's remains in and set them on the desk. She got very quiet and sat staring at the box for several moments. I waited with the paperwork until she seemed to come back from the moment, at which time she signed the papers.

She then picked up the box and commented, "Wow, it's much heavier than I thought it would be." I explained that, on average, cremated remains weigh between six and nine pounds.

About a week later, I received a call from the general manager, asking me to step into his office. I walked in and was offered a seat across from his large desk. I noticed upon entering the room that the case file for this woman's husband was on his desk. I looked at him curiously and asked, "What's going on?"

He held up the file on his desk and began. "We have a problem with this case."

"Oh?" I asked. I couldn't imagine what the problem could be since this had been such a simple case and everything seemed to go just perfectly.

He continued, "The wife advised me you need to be fired immediately for incompetence."

I looked at him, dumbfounded. My mind started racing. What could have possibly gone wrong that would make this woman have such a strong reaction?

Dan watched me as the display of emotions ran across my face. He continued, "Don't you want to know why?"

"Of course I do! What could have happened?"

"Well, when you brought the urn containing her husband's remains into the office, she suddenly felt extreme guilt for not having a funeral or memorial service. Also, she felt that she should have purchased a plot to have him interred."

"Um, okay. What has that got to do with me?" I asked.

"She insists that you should have told her how she was going to feel and advised her against the arrangements she chose."

What? How could I possibly know how anyone would react in the moment or, better yet, predict their feelings?

Dan looked at me again and smiled softly. "Don't worry, your job is safe, but you may need to take a course on mind-reading before you meet with any more families."

I smiled, relieved, and went back to work. To this day, I haven't gotten my degree in mind-reading or telling the future.

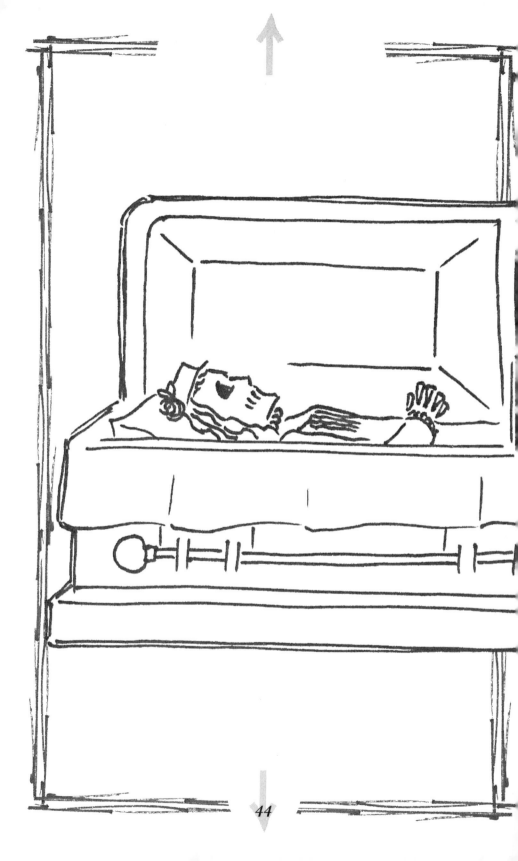

# The Annual Service

Whenever we arrange a service for a family, we try to make sure everything is explained before they leave the office so there are no unanswered questions later. A copy of all the paperwork is given to the family members with a full description of the service details so they can reference it instead of making unnecessary calls to the funeral director. Even with all of the double-checks and creative ways we have to ensure every base is covered before a service, inevitably you run across a family that requires just a little bit more attention than most. This was the case with a grieving mother whose son had just passed away after a long illness.

He and his twin brother, well into their thirties, still lived at home with their mother, and they all were obviously very close. The mother and brother were extremely emotional during the arrangements, and we received several calls on each of the days leading up to the service. In addition to the questions, the outpouring of emotion and anger was evident, but this is how some people deal with the loss of a loved one, and we try to not take it personally. This sometimes can be a challenge on the occasions when you are told daily everything you are doing is wrong or not good enough.

In this particular case, the family wanted a very lengthy obituary. This is not a problem, but when we informed the family that the newspaper would charge per line, they refused to pay the additional charges, so we went with the traditional obituary format the newspaper provides. The day the posting was printed, we received a phone call informing us that we had excluded the additional information they requested. Trying to explain that we had discussed this during the arrangement process was not working, as the mother insisted they had paid the additional charge for the printing. At these moments, I refer to the contract copy that we send home with the family so they can see exactly what was paid for and what was not included. The contract showed clearly there was no charge for this obituary, but even this did not convince the grieving mother.

Finally, the day of the service arrived, and the chapel was set up exactly to the specifications. Once the lengthy service concluded, the deceased was interred in an outside crypt, and the mourners departed. For the next several weeks, we would see the mother at the mausoleum crying and mourning the loss of her son. This is normal, and we have empathy for those in pain but do not get involved as mourning is a personal and private affair. For the next year, we continued to see mom regularly, along with the brother, bringing flowers and mementos to the crypt.

Now here's where things take a turn for the bizarre! Just a few days before the first anniversary of the death, the mother came into the mortuary and wanted to speak with the family service counselor who had made the arrangements the previous year. I escorted her into the office and informed the counselor that she was waiting for him. Within a short amount of time, we began to hear raised voices from the back office and went to investigate. Normally, funeral homes are very quiet places, so the sound of yelling will prompt investigation from the staff. Even with the door to the office closed, we could hear the anger and grief of this woman as she insisted that they hold a service for her son on the anniversary of his death. This is an unusual request, but it could be arranged. The problem was that the mother wanted an open casket! If you have never had the opportunity to research exactly what happens to a body after death, I can give you a brief synopsis.

During the first two hours, the blood begins to settle into the lowest part of the body, usually the back. Within eight hours, this becomes a permanent, irreversible stain to the skin. Rigor mortis (or stiffening of the body) begins within two hours of death; after twelve hours, the stiffness disappears, and the body becomes limp once again. After twenty-four hours, the decomposition stage begins. Within two or three days, intestinal gas buildup occurs, which smells like rotten eggs. This causes the body to bloat or swell, and the pallor of the skin turns from green to purple and finally to black during this period. Within a week, the skin begins to peel away from the muscle tissue, and the black discoloration has spread to the entire body.

After the second week, the body starts to become liquid as the cells break down even further. By the fourth week,

you are left with pretty much what you see in the old horror movies: a skeleton with hair and some skin left. The typical embalming process will only slow this process down slightly; within a month, you will see the same results.

With this in mind, you can clearly see why it would not be advisable for anyone to have a viewing of their loved one on an annual basis, even in the best circumstances. The counselor advised the mother that it would be better for everyone to remember her son the way he was, but she was insistent that the service would happen and said she would get a court order if necessary. When presented with a situation like this, you learn early on that it is best just to let things go. She left the mortuary, and we did not hear any more about a service but still did see her in the mausoleum quite frequently.

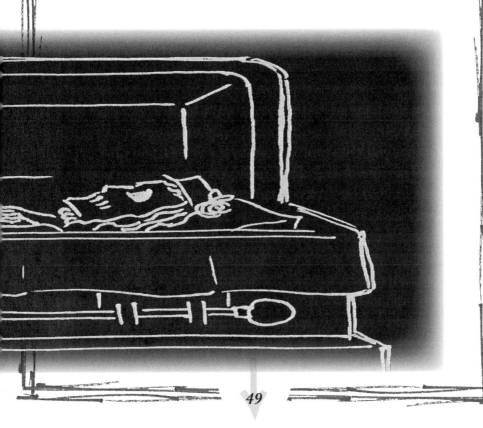

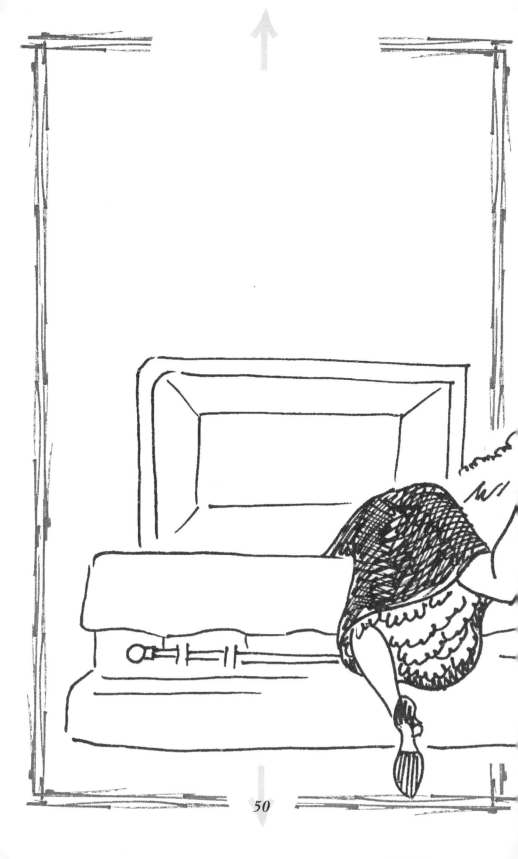

# Who Shot Whom?

I have said before that once you have been a family service counselor for a few years, you begin to feel like you have seen and done it all. Nothing could possibly shock or even surprise you. This is usually when life throws you a curve ball.

I received a homicide case in which the deceased had been shot several times. The wife was the legal next of kin, but she was hospitalized with multiple gunshot wounds also. Since the law at that time stated that only the wife could make the arrangements, we were going to have to wait until she was well enough to be discharged from the hospital. Therefore, I set the file aside until I heard from her.

The next day, I was asked to come to the lobby, as the wife had come to make arrangements. I quickly made my way to the front entrance, where I found a small woman standing alone with a ghostly white pallor to her skin. I introduced myself and assisted her to my office. I advised her that we could wait until she was well, but she insisted that this needed to be done in a hurry as the husband's parents were attempting to obtain power of attorney to make the funeral arrangements. My curiosity was getting the best of me; I was dying (no pun intended) to know how they both had been shot. As I began to organize the paperwork, she asked me, "Do you know how this happened?"

"No," I replied. Of course, I wanted to know. "Would you like to tell me?" I asked as diplomatically as I could.

She proceeded to tell me that she and her husband had gone to Las Vegas and gotten married very soon after meeting one another. They'd had a very volatile relationship from the beginning, but they were in love.

Some of the details she shared gave me the impression that perhaps drugs played a significant part in the lifestyle of this family. I continued to listen as she spun the story. The marriage continued to be difficult, and her husband had insisted several times that she was cheating on him. He had threatened her life on multiple occasions and also stated that he would rather kill her than have her leave him. On the evening in question, that is exactly what happened. He came home with gun in hand and shot her at point-blank range in the shoulder and in the side, leaving her wounded but still alive. Her nephew showed up just in time, and in the ensuing fight, her nephew fatally shot her husband.

I sat dumbfounded as I looked at this woman across the desk. This is the kind of thing you see in movies, but here it was, sitting in my office. I tried to quickly gain some composure. In the meantime, I asked her what kind of disposition she would like for the body. She wanted a simple cremation as they would be having a private service on their own afterward. In California, we are required to have a positive identification of the deceased before a cremation can take place. This is done for obvious reasons; we want to make sure we've got the right body before incinerating it. Identification can be performed by identifying the body in person or with a recent photo.

Most people go with the photo, but some prefer to see their beloved relative one last time. She opted to see the body, so I called the prep room and asked them to put him on a gurney in one of the viewing rooms. Within a few minutes, they were ready for us. I escorted her back to the visitation room, where I stood near the door while she slowly moved forward to examine the man who had attempted to kill her just days before. I'm not sure what I expected her to do at that moment, but I can assure you it was not even close to what actually took place.

I watched as she threw herself on the body of her husband and began sobbing uncontrollably. She began beating on his chest and crying out, "I love you! I forgive you! Please come back to me! Take me instead!" Now, for the ladies reading this, I can assure you that, if my husband ever decided to do me in and I survived and he didn't, I would not have the same reaction. I'm thinking the scene would more likely play out with me kicking the stretcher as I picked a few choice last words for him. That was not the case in this instance, and I stood quietly waiting for her to finish. Briefly, I was a little concerned that she would be injured further with the amount of force she was using in her grief. After a few minutes, the crying subsided, and we left the room. As I escorted her out, I explained, as I usually do, that the process would take three to four days, and I would contact her when it was complete.

You are probably thinking that the weirdness of this situation is over; I certainly did. We would both be wrong. The next day, I was working late when I was once again asked to come to the lobby. As I entered the front office, I saw a large group of people dressed in various stages of what could be described as Gothic black. I estimated about twenty people in the group, with the wife of the recently deceased at the front wearing a top hat complete with veil, a full-length black-lace dress, and high heels. She smiled at me and told me they had come to pick up her husband for the memorial. It was immediately apparent that this situation was about to go bad for me since there did not appear to be one person in this group in a sober state. I was feeling the anxiety and nervousness starting to build as I stood there, trying to figure out how to tell this entourage that the person they came to get was still sitting in the cooler.

I asked the woman to step into the office for a moment while the rest of the crowd found comfortable seating or leaned against walls. I tried to explain to her that the cremation had not been completed and that I had informed her that I would call when it was done. She blinked at me a couple of times and then got up to leave. No emotion or questions—just went back from where she had come with the rest of the party following like ducks in her wake. I really felt like I had dodged the proverbial bullet (no pun intended) on this one.

Several days later, I picked up the phone to let her know that her husband was ready for delivery. Later that day, she arrived, alone, with a T-shirt and sweatpants as her costume. She quietly picked up the urn and thanked me for my assistance. As I walked back to my office, I had to remind myself not to get too cocky in the future about having seen and heard it all. In this business, that's a surefire way to find yourself headed to new heights of bizarreness and insanity.

# The World's Oldest Funeral Director

Over the years, I met and worked with many people, most of them fairly forgettable. Not the case with one funeral director I worked with in the latter part of my career, Ralph Gordon. Ralph was a character from way back. He worked in the era when morticians made arrangements at the deceased's kitchen table—none of the formality required by today's world. He was from a time when everyone knew each other in the community, and they wouldn't call the mortuary. They would call the funeral director at home to come pick up the deceased. This was the age when the family would watch their loved one take that last breath in the comfort of their own bed.

This man had watched the funeral industry grow and change around him for the last fifty years, but he went with the times and seemed as happy today as he did in his earlier years. I loved to sit and listen to him tell stories about the funny and unusual events that took place in his life. Maybe someday I will document some of those great stories too.

Ralph's real charm was his quick wit. He could get a room full of people laughing and keep your mind absorbed in a story or joke. There was just one problem: He would tell you jokes at the most inappropriate moment.

When I made funeral arrangements with a family, I let them know that the funeral directing staff would be at the service to attend to anything they might need. I would come in just before the service to greet the family and to make sure everything was to their specifications.

Seeing a familiar face gave them a sense of reassurance. Ralph would stand just outside the chapel, handing out the memorial folders or asking those in attendance to sign the guest book. On one occasion, as I was about to walk into the chapel, Ralph motioned for me to come close and leaned in to whisper in my ear.

"I have something to tell you." I mistakenly made the assumption that this pertained to the service and listened intently.

"How was copper wire invented?" he asked and then paused for me to answer. When I just looked at him questioningly, he answered, "Two Jews pulling on a penny." My eyes widened and I held my breath, trying not to laugh out loud. How was I going to walk down the aisle and greet the family with that thought running around in my brain?

Somehow, I managed to follow through with my task and leave without losing my composure. When I got back to my desk I was seething, but at the same time terribly amused, that this old man had gotten me so good. I decided that next time I dealt with Ralph I would be better prepared and make sure he didn't get an opportunity to do the same.

The next time, I walked purposefully into the building, and there was Ralph, looking postured and serene in his suit. As I tried to breeze past him, he motioned for me again. "Sorry, Ralph. I'm in a hurry," I stated.

"No, this is important. Really," he re-plied.

He looked sincere, and I walked over to him.

"What do you get when you cross a potato with a penis? A dictator!"

He'd gotten me again! I couldn't believe this little man had lied to me just to try to fluster me once again. Now the gauntlet had been thrown. I would show this sneaky old man two could play this game. The next time I knew he would be at a service, I would be prepared.

Well, as fate would have it, he was not assigned to a service for another month, but when I saw his name assigned to a funeral, I made sure I would have my revenge.

The day of the service, I waited until five minutes before the conclusion and purposefully walked to the back of the building, where I knew he would be. Since this wasn't my arrangement, I didn't need to be concerned about what he would say, but wanted to get my dig in before he had to dismiss the mourners. I walked up to him and whispered in his ear, "What do you get when you take the insides out of a hotdog? A Halloweenie!" Without missing a beat, Ralph walked up the aisle to the front of the chapel and dismissed the service. He was totally unaffected by my joke.

Later that day, I was in the back of the office. This area is off-limits to the public, so we were free to chat and make some noise. I walked up to Ralph and shook his hand. He was the master and I the student of the funeral prank. Sometimes, you just need to bow before a great old funeral director.

# Is That Meant for One or Two?

I would not usually share this story due to the sensitive nature of the subject but, over the years, it has struck me as so funny that I felt compelled to share it.

We had a case later in my career of an oversized gentleman who had died suddenly. The family requested the body to be cremated. Unfortunately, California law disallowed the cremation of bodies over a certain amount of weight. Apparently, large amounts of body fat would cause fires within the oven and destroy the equipment. So the family was forced to purchase an oversized grave, vault, and casket for their loved one and have a traditional burial.

The family provided the clothing for the deceased, and the counselor took the garments up to the prep room so staff could prepare the deceased for the funeral. Meanwhile, another family I was working with brought in the clothing for their service, so I carried it down the hall and opened the heavy door leading to the prep area. What I saw then I will never forget as long as I live.

Two of the funeral directors were side by side in the middle of the room, each standing in one leg of this man's pants. Then, they put the coat around themselves, each putting one arm through a sleeve. I watched in disbelief as the embalmer snapped a picture with the instant camera they had for documentation of the bodies. Just about the time the flash of the camera went off, everyone turned and saw me standing behind them. The room quickly became very quiet, almost as if everyone was holding their breath. Clearly, they were waiting for me to say something or turn and run. I simply said, "Nice suit. Hope the tailor didn't get paid." Then I turned and left the room.

When something like this goes on, it is an innocent act, but still inappropriate. And the picture of the scene was eventually their downfall. News like this will always travel like wildfire in an office building, and this instance was no exception. By the next morning, there were whispers of the happenings all over the office. The fact that there was a photo made the story even juicier because everyone wanted to see it.

The story becomes even stranger because the photo had gone missing and no one involved seemed to know where it gotten to. Everyone naturally assumed that someone involved had taken it home. As it turns out, this was not the case.

Later that morning, the two guys who had been in the suit were called into the general manager's office. I was sitting in my office when I saw the two men walking by chatting in hushed tones to each other. One poked his head in and asked, "Did you say anything about what happened yesterday to anyone?"

"No," I said, "but it looks like I didn't need to. Everyone in the building knows the story."

"Well, we've been called to Dan's office."

"Good luck," I said as they walked off like two convicted criminals going to the gas chamber. I went back to my paperwork, wondering what would be the outcome for these two.

A short time later, here come the dynamic duo up the stairs and past my office. I called out, "Well, what happened?" I couldn't stand the suspense.

They looked at each other and then at me and began to tell the tale of their conversation with the boss:

They had walked in, and Dan, the office manager, asked them to sit down. He leaned back in his chair and tossed the Polaroid picture that had "gone missing" across the desk. They both looked at the photo and then at Dan in anticipation. He stared at them for a couple of moments and then asked, "Do you have anything to say about this?"

Both men gulped the knot of fear down but did not know what to say. Finally, one spoke up, "We didn't think it was a big deal at the time. It was just innocent fun. We never thought anyone would find out."

Dan folded his hands under his chin, contemplating the situation.

The two men could feel the sweat building up, their hearts beating out of their chests. Would they be fired, suspended, or worse?

It was evident by the look on the faces of the two men as I looked at them that they had gotten worse, but the incident was never spoken of again.

# In a Hurry to the Cemetery

Early in my career working in mortuaries, I was answering phones and setting appointments for the family service counselors. This was a busy job on most days, but occasionally the phones would be very quiet. This particular day, it seemed like the entire world had dropped away. It was just too quiet in the office. Only one service was scheduled, and it was an offsite service, so there was almost no one in the building.

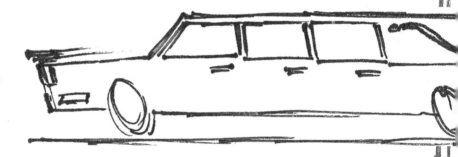

Late in the afternoon, the phone finally rang. I answered it and was surprised when the California Highway Patrol was on the other end. The man on the phone was very direct when he asked for the manager of the establishment. I put the officer on hold and rang my boss's office to pick up the call. The other people in the office heard my end of the call and came in to see what was going on.

"Who was that?" asked one of my colleagues.

"The Highway Patrol wants to talk with the boss. I hope nothing has happened."

The anticipation was palpable while we waited to find out the reason for the call. When the boss came out of his office, we all held our breath waiting for the news.

I don't think I had ever seen this man's face so red before. For a moment, I thought his veins would pop out of his head he was so angry.

"Do you want to know what that was about?" he asked.

The thought I had was, "Duh, of course." But that is not what came out of my mouth. I said as calmly and disinterestedly as I could muster, "Sure. What's going on?"

"That idiot Jay was clocked driving down the highway at speeds over 100 miles an hour! I'm going to kill him when he gets back!" And he stormed out of my office to the front of the building.

Now, I have to admit the first question that came to my mind upon hearing this was, "Did he have the funeral party following the hearse?" That would be quite a sight, seeing a line of cars twenty deep with escorts flying down the freeway on the way to the cemetery. Did he get pulled over with the casket still in the back of the funeral coach?

When Jay returned to the office with the hearse, we all sat back and waited for the fireworks to start. He seemed happy and relaxed as he entered the building. This would not last long. Clearly, the boss heard the door open and came into the room with steam coming out of his ears. "I got a call from the police that you were speeding in the hearse. Get into my office NOW!" The look on Jay's face went from pleasure to instant terror as he looked around and then slowly followed the enraged man down the hallway.

What seemed like hours (but was really more like a few minutes) passed before he reappeared, looking like he had been beaten over the head with a large stick. He looked up and saw us waiting for him to say something and he began, "I was clocked doing 100 miles per hour in the hearse on the way back from the cemetery. The police said they would have normally taken me in for reckless driving, but they weren't sure if it was an emergency or not."

We all started to laugh. What kind of emergency would cause a hearse to speed? It's not like someone's dying or sick!

# Eternity in Bondage

The issue of clothing for a deceased is pretty much the same for every family. The majority of the time, they don't think to bring something with them when they come to make arrangements, so another trip to the funeral home is required to bring in an outfit. This particular day, the family brought in everything Mom would need to be dressed appropriately for the service. I usually don't check the contents since I give them a list ahead of time of the garments that we will require.

I brought the bag of clothing to the prep room, marked the name of the deceased on the outside, and left, not thinking about it again.

I was sitting in my office when someone knocked. It was the embalmer, standing there looking uncomfortable.

"I found something in the bag I'm not sure what do to with."

"What is it?" I asked with trepidation. What could possibly be included that he would be confused about?

"Do you know what this is?" He held up a piece of clothing I had not seen since I was a child. It was an old-fashioned girdle. My eyes widened as I let out a laugh.

"That's a girdle. Women wear them to hold everything in so they look slimmer. Can you imagine going through eternity in that thing?" I said, barely able to catch my breath.

For you ladies who have ever attempted to put on a girdle, you know that it can be a challenge. Try to imagine squeezing, tugging, and pulling this device on a body that cannot assist.

The embalmer looked at me again and asked the question, "How am I supposed to get this thing on her?"

"I have no idea, but good luck," I said teasingly.

"Would you please call the family and ask them if I really need to put this thing on her?"

"Okay, I'll check for you, but if they say it goes on, you're going to have to shoehorn it on her." He looked at me as if to say, "Not funny." Then he turned and walked out of my office.

I pulled the contact information from the file and called the next of kin to inquire about the garment. When I asked the son if they really wanted it on their mother, his response was, "She never left the house without it on. She would want to look her best at the service."

Very often during these times, people don't really stop to think about what they are saying, but even so it was not my job to contradict their wishes. I thanked him for letting me know and assured him that it would be with her.

I walked into the prep room and saw the embalmer sitting at his desk with the formidable garment hanging behind him on a hook. He looked up from his paperwork and stared at me expectantly.

"Well, they said she never leaves the house without it, and they want her to look her best at the service." I just couldn't help the laugh that escaped when I finished the sentence.

He looked at me like I had informed him he was being executed in the morning.

"Look, all I told them was it would be with her. I didn't say it would be on her. Just make sure she looks like she has it on in case they check."

His eyes lit up with relief, and then suddenly looked puzzled. "Do you think they would really check?"

"I hope not, but you never know. Stranger things have been known to happen."

The last I heard, the service went perfectly, and the family was very pleased that mother went to her reward with her girdle firmly in place.

# Funeral for a Homey

In the Southern California area, we have the misfortune to have a large gang population. With this comes the sad reality of gang violence. The funeral industry is laden with young kids who have died far too young in shootings or other acts of violence.

On this occasion, a young Mexican boy around fifteen years old was brought to our funeral home after being shot by a rival gang. The distraught mother and father came to us to make the arrangements and requested that no obituary be posted, no information be given out to the public, and additional security be available for the service so his gang member friends would not be able to attend. We were happy to comply with their wishes and made the arrangements to be certain that the final memorial would be as peaceful as possible.

One day prior to the service, the mortuary was quietly conducting business as usual, and I was taking advantage of the relative quiet to catch up on paperwork. I was standing near the lobby when a large group of young boys in their early teens walked into the office and stood around the receptionist desk. One tall young man, who looked to be the leader, stood in the middle and demanded to know if their "homey" was there. The girl behind the desk tried in vain to tell the boys that we had no information. Meanwhile, this poor girl was trying not to convey the terror she was feeling from being confronted by this group of gangsters.

As I continued to watch the scene play out, I realized a small group of my coworkers was gathering behind me.

The staff had realized there was something amiss and had gathered here to get a front-row seat for the show. About fifteen people, mostly male, watched from the protection of a nearby glassed and walled office while this girl was trying to deal with this issue. She knew, as we did, that she could not give out the information but clearly was terrified of what might happen if they decided to force the issue.

Some fifteen years later, I am still not sure if it was fear for Tiffany's safety or the disgust I felt for the men standing behind me that triggered me to act. Regardless of the motivation, I gathered up my courage, stepped quickly toward Tiffany, and asked the gang of boys if I could help them. Even in the state I was in, I had the presence of mind to tell one of my colleagues to call the police just before I left to confront the gang. This way, at least we would have some assistance in the event that something did go badly.

I immediately noticed two things. First, these kids were wearing pants that showed most of their buttocks, and second, the leader of the group had the butt end of a handgun protruding from the belt of his trousers. I also couldn't help but notice the fact that the gun seemed to be slipping lower as the discussion continued until only an inch or so of the handgrip was showing. It was apparent to me that he would never be able to get his hand around the weapon fast enough to fire it, and, more than likely, it would fall out the bottom of his pant leg.

I've always been one to find humor in a situation, and this really was very funny to me. I knew better than to laugh and antagonize these young men who were working hard to intimidate their way into getting what they wanted. It was a battle they were destined to lose.

Almost as if the leader of this pack of boys could read my mind, he moved his hand up toward the waistband of his blue jeans and reached for his gun. As if on cue, the gun slipped down and disappeared, causing a noticeable bulge where the legs began. He continued to reach into his pants, trying desperately to retrieve the runaway pistol without success.

Fortunately for everyone involved, the local police arrived and marched in to break up the party. The last I saw of these kids, the front man was being dragged out the front doors, trying to retrieve the wayward gun.

Thankfully for the family and friends, the service for the young man was as close to perfect as they could have hoped for. None of the group from the incident the day before showed up.

# Glitterati for Mama

Many times when meeting with a family to make arrangements for a memorial, I am handed an insurance policy to pay for the funeral expenses. This is a perfectly acceptable arrangement for most funeral homes once the policy has been verified with the insurance carrier. It eases the burden on the family financially and makes the services run much more smoothly for everyone involved.

On this particular day, I walked out to the lobby to meet with a large group of family members who had come in to make arrangements for their deceased mother. As I sat with this obviously caring family, we created a memorial fit for royalty: only the best of everything for their loving mother. The gravesite was in an older, more mature part of the cemetery with lots of shade trees. They chose the finest bronze casket with silk lining and vault to match, and the memorial stone was the finest-quality granite. Of course, they required dozens of arrangements of flowers to send their mother off with great fanfare. Last but not least, after the large church service, six white stretch limousines would carry Mom and her extensive family to the gravesite, where white doves would be released at the end of the graveside service. When everything was finally selected, the total for service came to nearly twenty-five thousand dollars.

As a family service counselor, I was paid a commission. Therefore, a funeral of this magnitude was financially lucrative for me as well as for the funeral home. As with any family I met with, the issue of payment was one of the last items on the checklist since full payment was required prior to any services being rendered. The oldest of the woman's children, a very well-dressed man in his fifties, came forward and produced from his papers an insurance policy. I smiled politely as I explained the process of how the insurance policy would be used to pay for the services, and then I escorted the group to the lobby. Everyone left the meeting with a sense that this funeral would be an event to remember. Once the planning session was complete, I started preparations, delivering the necessary paperwork to the prep room, clerical, florist, and, of course, accounting staff.

Later that day, I received a knock on my office door and looked up to see one of our new employees from accounting standing nervously in my doorway with a stack of paperwork in his hand. I asked, "What can I do for you?" He walked in and sat across from me, looking stricken.

"Did you have a chance to look at this policy before the family left?" he asked.

I admitted that I had not.

This nervous young man then placed the stack of papers on my desk and slowly pushed it toward me. I held it up and began reading what most would call a dry, boilerplate insurance policy with the names and amounts filled in. After a few seconds, he asked me to look at the date the policy was issued. My eyes nearly bulged out of my head when I saw the date. Only two months had elapsed between the issue date and the date of death.

It was obvious to me and the accountant that something fishy was going on with these arrangements.

Without hesitation, I picked up the phone on my desk and called the contact number on the contract. It was company policy that no service would be rendered until payment was made in full, for the obvious reason that once a funeral has been held, it is almost impossible to get the money. Nervously, I waited for the party on the other end to pick up but was left disappointed when I was connected to a voicemail. I left a message asking for the responsible party to contact me.

Several hours later, the receptionist informed me that one of the family members was on the phone, and I eagerly picked up the call. I had been wondering how to handle the situation without causing further turmoil at this difficult time. It was the eldest son on the line, and I explained to him as delicately as possible that the insurance policy was not going to cover the funeral expenses since the insurer requires substantial time to pass before honoring the payment. Several seconds of silence passed before he said that he would need to call me back.

Certainly, I could understand the concern of a family that had just spent an enormous amount of money picking out the perfect farewell for a loved one. I hung up the phone certain that they would be able to work out the payment and went back to working on other services.

It wasn't until I left work that night and got into my car that I suddenly realized that I had not received a return phone call. I went home, knowing there was nothing to be done about it until the next day.

Upon my arrival at work the following morning, I had several messages but nothing regarding the arrangement in question. Accounting was looking for me as soon as I entered the building, but I had no update for them regarding the payment. Everything would remain on hold until I could make another call.

It was mid-morning when I was finally able to clear my desk and make another call. Once again, no answer, and I left my name and number asking for a return call.

To my surprise, only minutes later, several members of the woman's family walked in the front door. I naturally assumed that they were going to take care of the payment personally and was thrilled to see their faces.

I escorted them back to the office once again, pulled the file and sat down to finish what had been started the day before. Figuring they were going to write the check, I pulled the contract out of the file and looked up. The man across from me smiled politely and cleared his throat before speaking. "We have decided go ahead and cremate Mama and cancel the service," he said.

I looked at the man for a second before forming my response. "So, you would like a direct cremation without a memorial service instead of the package you chose yesterday?"

"Yes, that is correct."

I was unsure what to say at this point but went ahead and rewrote the contract per their request, the grand total coming to eleven hundred dollars. He wrote a check, and they left the office. As I walked them out to the lobby, I felt like I had to ask. "Excuse me, sir. What made you change your mind about the service you had selected yesterday?"

"Oh, we just figured on the insurance paying off so we wouldn't have to pay for anything. When we found out they wouldn't pay, we just figured it wasn't worth it."

Sometimes I am sorry to have asked the question that should never have been answered.

# The Garbage Man Delivery

A few months after I started working with families on making funeral arrangements, we hired on a new funeral director. This man had just completed his service in the United State Marines and was looking for work to support his wife and new daughter. He was eager to learn we found him to be a pleasant man to work with.

In a small facility as was this first place I worked, sometimes you jump in and help out anywhere work needs to be done. This particular day, the new guy was assisting the yard crew with cleaning up an area of the cemetery that was in bad need of weeding. He had put on his grey coveralls and work boots and got to work, sweating in the heat of the day.

In the office, we received a call from another mortuary asking us to pick up a body from their facility. The family had decided to work with us and we needed to come get the deceased and schedule a meeting with the family.

The receptionist got the information and radioed out to the yard for them to send in our funeral director to go make the pickup.

He came into the office, hot and sweaty and got the information where he was to be going and then left the office through the prep room door. We all naturally assumed he would shower and change clothes prior to leaving so he would be presentable upon his arrival at the other funeral home.

Unfortunately, this was not to be the case. The old boy jumped immediately into the van and took off without giving a thought to his appearance. Meanwhile, the rest of the staff went back to work thinking our guy was handling everything.

A few hours later, we received a call from the other funeral home. The director of their mortuary was laughing so hard into the phone I could hardly understand what was being said.

"I love that you send your garbage man to pick up bodies for you," he said teasingly into the phone.

"I don't understand what you're talking about," I replied. Then it suddenly hit me. Our man had not changed his clothing. I quickly apologized for the unprofessionalism of our man and explained it would not happen again.

Just about this time, the van pulled into the garage and the funeral director jumped out, still dirty and in his coveralls.

"So, how did it go for the pick up?" I asked.

"Fine, they sure acted funny when I got there though," he said.

"Why do you suppose they were 'acting funny?'" I asked, trying to lead him to the correct conclusion.

"I don't know; they just seemed awfully amused the whole time I was there."

I then asked him to follow me into the prep area and stood him in front of the mirror.

"Have you looked in a mirror since you were asked to pick up the body?"

"Gosh, I look pretty bad, huh?"

"Yes, you do. Do me a favor and make sure you clean yourself up and change next time there's a call."

It was many, many years before we lived that stunt down.

# I Dare You To Open It

Regularly, when you work with the dead, you receive a body that has successfully committed suicide. Sometimes they hang themselves, take pills, use a gun, or many other variously creative ways of doing the deed.

Once in a while, you meet one that has truly done the job in the most quick and effective way they could find. This person decided to step in front of a train. While this is a very fast way to die, it is also the messiest, as the body tends to be broken into several parts and the coroner's office ends up delivering the body to us in a plastic bag, rather than on a gurney.

The bag of remains sat on a shelf in the cooler for two days before news got around the office as to what was inside. Several of the funeral counselors were curious to see what the cooler contained, but did not have the bravery to actually ask the prep staff to open it.

I on the other hand knew someone on the inside. My husband was on the funeral director's staff and worked very closely with the prep team. So I walked into the office and asked him if they had peeked inside the bag of remains.

"No, not yet," he replied.

"Are you going to?" I asked.

"Well, let's see." He got up and stuck his head into the embalming room and asked the people working in there if anyone wanted to take a look at the jigsaw puzzle body.

Only two people came out as David opened the door to the cooler and wheeled out the now infamous bag of body parts. It sat on the table at an odd sort of angle as the four of us stood surrounding it.

"There it is," I said.

"Go ahead, David, open it," said Lisa.

"I'm not opening it; you open it," replied David.

"I'm not going to open it."

"Why don't you open it, Catherine," said John the embalmer.

"Hey, don't get me involved in this. I just asked if you guys had opened it yet."

For some of you older folks reading this. The scene was very reminiscent of the Life Cereal® commercial with Mikey. "You try it. I'm not gonna try it, you try it."

"Hey, let's get Mikey; he'll eat anything." Like a bunch of little kids, we were all afraid of what we were going to see.

As I stood staring at the bag, my mind began to imagine all of the different configurations the body parts could be in. How many would there be? How large or small? Could they be identified or would they just be hunks of meat like at the butcher shop.

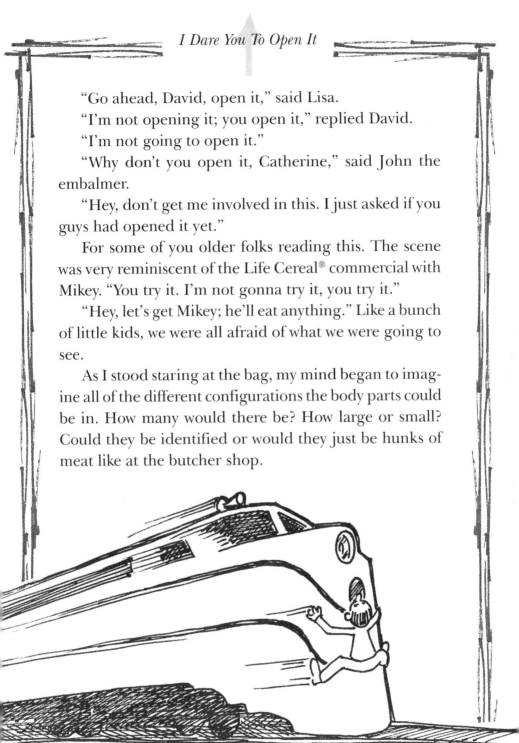

Finally Lisa broke the silence, "Look you guys, I need to get back to work, so if we're going to do this, let's get it done."

This was my opportunity to get out of there without having to see anything. "I really need to get back to work, too. Let me know what you find in the bag," I said as I backed quickly out of the room.

Later that evening, David came into my office and sat down.

"Did you guys finally open the bag?" I asked.

"No, we all chickened out," he replied.

The body was finally cremated and I still wonder to this day what that lady looked like in that bag on the shelf.

# Suicide: How Would You Want to Go?

I n this business, the talk of how people die is a frequent subject in the lunch room and around the water cooler. On this particular day, we had a body arrive in which the man had tried to hang himself. He had dressed up in his best blue jeans, cowboy shirt, belt buckle, and hat, pulled the rope around his neck, and jumped. Unfortunately for him, judging from the state he was in when he arrived, it was immediately apparent that he had neither a quick nor peaceful end. Strangulation was the cause of death instead of a broken neck.

Suicide is not uncommon these days, but the way in which people attempt to kill themselves becomes more and more creative. One guy jumped from the top of a building only to land on his feet and become about four inches shorter than when he started. One lady just stepped in front of a train, forcing the county coroner to use a garbage bag instead of a body bag to collect the remains. While there is a certain morbid curiosity about seeing a human body after it has been hit by a train, none of us were brave enough to open the bag of parts that remained of her when she arrived.

On another day, as we all ate our sandwiches and sipped our soda, the topic of conversation again turned to suicide: How would you do it? Several of my co-workers felt that gassing themselves with car exhaust fumes would be a peaceful way to go. This was, of course, before learning that the gasses cause a lovely purplish hue to the skin that is irreversible.

We ruled out hanging, since the odds of the neck breaking were slim (as evidenced by the dead cowboy). I certainly don't like the idea of being hanged by my neck waiting to strangle to death.

Next was drugging. While this might be the least violent way to go, the possibility of your body rejecting the drugs, vomiting all over yourself, and then having to start over just doesn't appeal to me.

The next one was drowning. Let's face it, folks: this would never happen. No matter how badly you want to die, the survival instinct would be too strong and you'd be back up at the top in no time.

On down the list we went, rejecting several more. Step in front of a train? Too messy. Shoot yourself? Too much possibility of missing. Jumping off something (building, bridge, cliff, etc.)? Afraid of heights.

The final conclusion was that there just isn't any good way of doing yourself in, so why not just enjoy the ride you're on and make the most out of your life.

# Suicide Throughout History

For those of you curious about how others decided to end things a little early, let's look at some of the more notable suicides throughout history.

Early Christians, like the Donatists and the Circumcellions, jumped off cliffs because of the promise of a great afterlife. When the church noticed that fewer and fewer people were showing up for services and the collection plate was getting smaller, they outlawed this practice and instead told people they would go to hell if they succeeded in their efforts to take their own lives.

Buddhism, Hinduism, and Confucianism all supported suicide in cases where there was incurable disease.

In ancient Egypt, suicide was considered as natural as living. They believed that, since you are only passing from this life to the next, there was no big deal.

In Japan, certain forms of suicide are considered honorable. Hari-kari is the act of thrusting a jeweled dagger into one's own vital organs to prompt death. And Kamikaze pilots would fly their planes into a target and thus be considered great warriors for this act.

In nineteenth-century Europe, a military man who could not pay his gambling debts would be encouraged to commit suicide to avoid dishonor.

In ancient China, India, and Egypt, the widow of a dead man was expected to jump into the funeral pyre so she could be reunited with her husband in the afterlife.

The practice was called "suttee." Interesting note here: Only the women were required to perform this act; no record of men doing the same for their dead wives.

In more recent history, the followers of Jim Jones in Guyana drank a cocktail of Kool-Aid laced with poison. Over 900 people died that day, but Jim decided against following his people's example and instead shot himself and his wife.

In California, the Heaven's Gate cult decided to hitch a ride on the Hale Bopp comet to go to the afterlife all together, thirty-nine total with their sneakers on.

# Stranger Than Fiction

O ver the years, I have collected a great library of books on the subject of death. I have come to the conclusion that truth is most certainly stranger than fiction. Whether you choose to believe them or not, here is a sampling of some of the stories I have collected about fitting endings.

# Going Down?

A man in Poland came home and informed his wife he was leaving her and left the apartment they had shared together for their entire marriage. The woman became so distraught after he left she jumped from the window of their tenth-story home. As fate would have it, her husband was coming out the front door of the building when she landed on him, killing him. The wife survived.

# High Price to Pay

Hrand Arakelin was working for an armored truck company. He was not killed at the hands of thieves holding up the truck to steal money. Arakelin left this life after the truck he was riding in the back of swerved, causing fifty thousand dollars in quarters to shift, thereby crushing him.

# Making a Clean Killing

Pat Burke, a homeless man in St. Louis, Missouri, was admitted to the city hospital and died. What did he die of, you ask? Because Burke hadn't bathed for twenty years, the hospital staff scrubbed him with brooms, which caused a skin infection that went untreated.

# Cats Really Do Have Nine Lives

Henri Villette decided to get rid of an unwanted cat so he tied the animal in a sack, planning on throwing it in the river by his home in France. Villette slipped, fell into the water along with the cat, and drowned. The cat managed to escape the bag and swim to safety.

# Too Strange to Be True

Charles Doak, president of the Wilson Candy Company didn't see his end coming when he arrived for work that day. He was beaten to death with a ninety-pound candy cane.

Mazar Zia drowned when she fell into a vat of gravy while on the job.

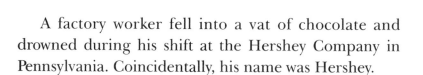

A factory worker fell into a vat of chocolate and drowned during his shift at the Hershey Company in Pennsylvania. Coincidentally, his name was Hershey.

David Grundman was crushed by the very cactus that he was shooting at in the Arizona desert. Grundman was taking target practice with the cactus when it brought sweet revenge on the man.

King Henry IV of England died of fright, having once been told by a fortune teller that he would die in Jerusalem. The king went into an epileptic fit at Westminster Abbey and was resting comfortably when he was informed the room was called the Jerusalem room. The shock killed him instantly.

King Ferdinand V of Spain was informed by a fortune teller that he would die in Madrigal. The king took great care to make sure to never visit the town. He became ill in a small village and died from terror when he was told that the town was called Little Madrigal.

Author Jonathan Swift wrote a book called, *Predictions of the Year 1708*, under the pseudonym Isaac Bickerstaff. In the book, he predicted the death of John Partridge, a competing author. When Partridge did not accommodate the writer by dying on time, Swift published a small pamphlet stating that the death had occurred as predicted. The document went on to say that Partridge also admitted on his deathbed to being a fake. Partridge took out a newspaper ad, letting the public know he was in fact still alive and the story was completely false. He lived for seven more years but spent most of those years trying to prove his identity. He died never knowing who Bickerstaff really was.

# Conclusion

While these are just a few of the tales told about the incredible mishaps that plagued me during my years in the business of death and burial, I have no doubt there are thousands more just like it.

If you cracked a smile or raised an eyebrow in disbelief, then I've succeeded in my task to show that there can be laughable moments when saying goodbye to a loved one.

When all is said and done, it is the memory we carry in our hearts and in our smiles that matters most.

~Catherine Olen